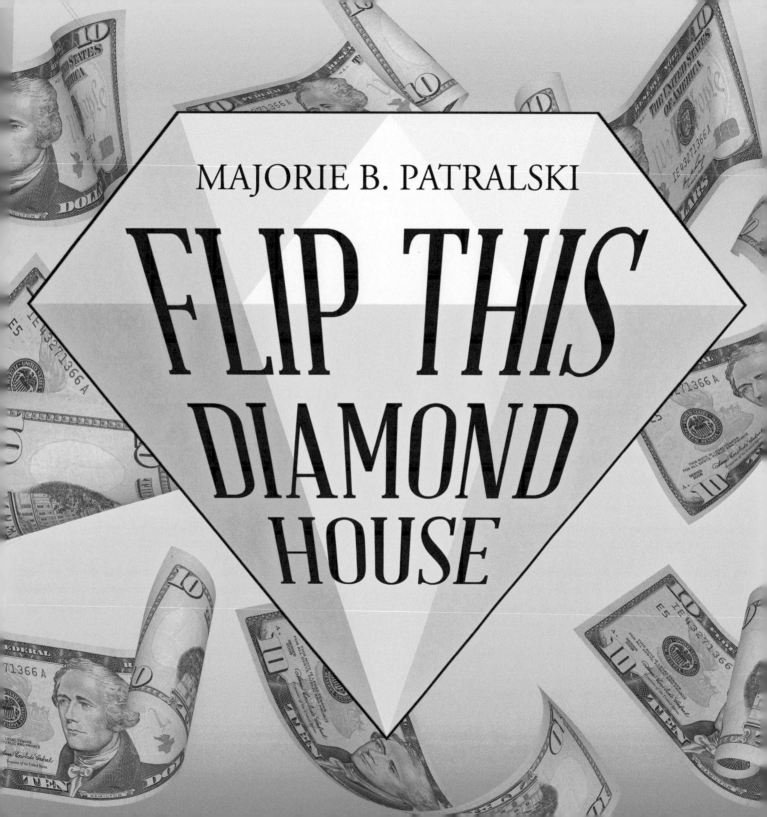

Balboa Press books may be ordered through booksellers or by contacting:

Balboa Press
A Division of Hay House
1663 Liberty Drive
Bloomington, IN 47403
www.balboapress.com
1 (877) 407-4847

ISBN: 978-1-9822-2346-5 (sc)
ISBN: 978-1-9822-2347-2 (e)

Library of Congress Control Number: 2019902826

Print information available on the last page.

Balboa Press rev. date: 03/15/2019

BALBOA.
PRESS
A DIVISION OF HAY HOUSE

TABLE OF CONTENTS

Why a Diamond

Today you have made the decision to open this book and read about how to properly flip a *diamond house*. Well, it's not literally a diamond house, but maybe something similar to one after its true colors are revealed. You have made the decision to find a goal to accomplish. You have pondered this great idea of purchasing this property, whether it's your first or not, and making magic happen. *Why a diamond house?* you may be asking. Well, because every house you find and dedicate yourself to, every house that you make shine and light up, and every house you polish and give brilliance to on that street is awakened and should be considered a diamond. Why? Because of the lasting life you will give it. Remember, diamonds are forever.

This is not your ordinary house-flipping book. This book will give you reliable information, offer true situations that you may be faced with, and provide awesome firsthand advice on how to achieve what you have sought out to do. I have included several tools in each chapter to help in your house-flipping process, as well as real pictures of one of my diamond flip houses. There are certain questions that you should always ask yourself in your evaluation process when getting ready to purchase a house, and I have included those tips and tools as well.

I do not have all the answers, and you may not even agree with some of my advice, but as long as you can carry away even one thing learned to help you accomplish your goal, then I am thrilled. Reading this book will definitely be worth the effort if even just one of my photos gives you a great idea for one of your houses and is enough to aim you in the right direction. In this treasure-hunting career path or hobby of flipping houses, we all need to continuously strive to learn new tips and push ourselves to keep going. I believe completely in "seeing is believing," and with colored pictures and tools to help us, we as humans can accomplish anything. I have included fifty splendid colored photos to help give you a better idea of how a house can become that diamond in the rough, sparkling and shining.

This information will give you more knowledge regarding the bumps and obstacles that are involved with house flipping. My goal is to be able to share the truth about house flipping with as many people as possible so that everyone who is ready to flip a diamond house will be able to do so with confidence and power to fulfill their dreams. All of our goals can be accomplished merely through thinking they can happen and pushing along the path to get there. We have to instill in our minds at the beginning of any task, whether small or big, that we will succeed and make this the best darn thing we can do. Your mind's energy will put the belief into place for you. If you visualize the project as nearly complete, that you just need to take the steps to get to the end, then it will make your goal seem more effortless, more rewarding, and more hobby oriented instead of a task that needs to be fulfilled.

We as humans must learn first, gather knowledge and wisdom, and then put these into action to be able to excel at our dreams and goals. That's right—those will be your first steps to house flipping, even before you find the house.

Stop and take a deep breath, relax, and say to yourself, "The knowledge I will gather will completely steer me in the most positive direction." Then not only will this knowledge steer you in the most positive direction, but also it will steer you directly into your first house to flip—and every one thereafter. The homes will begin to feel almost as though a magnet is pulling you closer; before you know it, every home that you flip will begin to have some of the same qualities as the previous one and the one before that. In addition, we tend to gravitate at times to homes that remind us of a pleasant moment in our lives, a memory that brings on a good feeling or vibe. And then *bam*, unexpectedly, you will start to pick your homes, or as I say, they will start to pick you.

This book will be a short but sweet book—one of those easy-to-read types packed with a lot of information in a small number of pages. Those types of books allow us to skim through them with little effort, pull out what we need for ourselves, compare it with others' opinions, and then put it to work right away without wasting any of our valuable time. As you will quickly realize as an investor, time is so valuable—and time literally is money. After you have gathered your knowledge, you are in the next position to once again relax and allow your natural wisdom to take over and be your guide for the next few months of your project.

Intelligence and physical strength are not the only things needed to build and fix things. Knowledge and wisdom are also such important key factors in this business or hobby that you are pursuing. These important gifts will help in this endeavor and in every aspect of your life as you make things run smoothly and with such ease and energetic vibration.

By using these tools, things will start to fall into place all around you. You will bring all the right people around you to help you actively with your project; you will deter all problems and handle obstacles with ease and grace. This will come to you from the knowledge that you gathered prior to starting and then by your natural wisdom.

Wisdom will respond to your complete comfort level positively because of the amount of knowledge you have gained prior to starting. In the next chapter, we will discuss gathering knowledge and awakening your natural wisdom. These are the crucial first steps to locating the right house and getting it for the right price.

One of the most important things to remember when flipping a house is to flip it correctly and properly. Chapter 5 will provide information on flipping houses properly, and this information can ultimately make or break your house-flipping dreams.

We need to remember that things done correctly will always be rewarded in due time.

We will look at profits as well as how to maximize them. We are not discussing the little profits that people earn for a side part-time job. Hard work, sweat, and mistakes turn into five to ten thousand dollars at the end of the flip. If you are putting in all the time and effort to think about your dream and then all the time and effort to put your dream into action, you must make sure you will be rewarded. You should have enough funds to outlast your stress during the process.

In this book, you will learn how to earn larger profits from house flipping and not settle for a month or two of paid bills. You will learn how to earn a twenty- to thirty-thousand-dollar profit every time. You will learn a lot of pointers and tips. Later, in chapter 3, we will start to look at the difference in spending and how to maximize profit.

I have put together real numbers used to buy and sell my properties, true numbers that can be used for your comparison purposes when looking at properties. Now, not all states' and cities' property values are similar, but by familiarizing yourself with the estimated numbers I have provided, it will help you gain more knowledge for negotiation and the house-flipping process. These numbers, facts, proposals, estimates, and situations can be used to get the most out of every flip.

By the time you read this chapter, it will be like turning on a light in a dark room. Normally it is so hard to get real numbers to look at, but in this book, I will share some of mine with you to use as tools.

I am ready to dive in and start showing you the ins and outs of flipping a diamond house. If you read this book from start to finish, you will surely be on the path to success with your house-flipping goal.

Gathering Knowledge and Using Your Natural Wisdom

I have to say that these will be your most important steps to making the house-flipping process go as smoothly as possible.

First let's look a little at two gifts: knowledge and wisdom. In the dictionary, knowledge is defined as an acquaintance with facts or principles. We can then automatically see how important it is to achieve our goals of house flipping.

Wisdom is obviously the quality of being wise, knowledge of what is true and right combined with just enough judgment. Aha! The two go hand in hand so one can be acquired with the other.

Knowledge is a most important quality to have, for it is used in everyday living and helps us get through our day. There are different characteristics of knowledge that help us accomplish different things in life. As we go through each day, we are using different types of knowledge to be able to take action correctly in this world. What we use frequently is basic knowledge and learned or acquired knowledge.

Basic knowledge includes all the basic things we know and have learned to be able to function properly. We have the knowledge to stop at a red light, to tie our shoes before walking, and to get up for work at a certain time. Using the basic functions on a day-to-day basis, we have become accustomed to these, so they have been formed and exercised properly. In some parts of the world, these would not be considered basic knowledge since they are not ever taught or used.

Then we have our learned or acquired knowledge, which is what sets us apart from everyone around us and makes each person an individual. This type of knowledge is truly amazing to have because the amount of knowledge we acquire or learn is the amount of intelligence we must be able to acquire wisdom and what we want in life. Our lives' goals and dreams begin to form and are put into action with this type of knowledge.

We are taught about certain subjects or idea in schools and from books as well as with experience and hands-on projects. We begin to gather information about that idea and know this idea or subject has officially become knowledge in our minds; it has officially filled our minds, having been implanted there for a time. Depending on how interesting this idea or subject is to us is how long it actually remains our learned knowledge.

For example, when I was a child, I had a rough childhood. My parents were very poor; they had come from Europe to the United States in the 1980s, seeking a better life and freedom from communism. At this time, they did not know the language and had no choice but to learn it to be able to live here and fit into society.

I also had to learn, and learning was never my favorite thing in school. I had a hard time and would actually walk out of my classes if I did not understand something or was not interested, so in those subjects, I did not acquire knowledge. Algebra and math were always my least favorite subjects, so I never learned those. Never to this day have I had an idea how to do an algebraic equation, nor do I want to learn algebra.

This shows us that if the idea or subject is not important to us or will not become us or shape us, it will not become knowledge that we retain for a long time. It either will become temporary knowledge or will never even be learned. What we need to focus on in life is finding the knowledge all the way back from childhood that becomes who we are today and helps shape us into prosperous and healthy individuals.

When I began buying and flipping houses, I had this passion for it, this push that said, "Do this because you want to learn about it and feel it." An excitement burst inside of me, and I began to want to know everything about the process of flipping houses. I began to research day and night about how to start. I began to gather knowledge about flipping houses from every place I could—watching shows, reading books, and driving neighborhoods that were being flipped. It was a knowledge I wanted to acquire, and it began to shape me. The passion had been awakened, and there was no stopping me.

This type of knowledge is the best; it becomes easy to acquire because we are interested in acquiring it. Not everyone can flip houses—or maybe they will flip but not continue because this is not their passion. If it is something that is not truly inside ourselves and we don't have a passion for it, it will be hard to learn the knowledge accurately and hard to shape us to follow that idea or subject. This is when it becomes just that, an idea and subject rather than a dream or goals.

Any type of learned knowledge that has benefited us or helped us learn something that we did not previously know and made us wiser becomes wisdom. Wisdom is a gift that needs to be taken seriously and needs to be listened to in order to reproduce more of it and keep that gift strong. It is a never-ending gift with unlimited potential and needs to be respected and put to use to benefit us and others around us. When used correctly, wisdom will help thousands of people we meet or interact with and will heal, support, guide, and purify. Wisdom will only be given to those who seek it with honest, earnest hearts. This will be discussed more in chapter 6, "Make or Break Your Goals."

So when we find our passion to flip houses, this will always be our first step to gather knowledge. We must know that the process takes time and will have different obstacles to overcome, but if we do our research ahead of time, it will ultimately get us doing exactly what we are dreaming of doing.

CHAPTER 3

Do Your Research

Research is essential to being able to locate the correct property you are looking for. Flipping houses is commonly mistaken as something that can be done quickly and with minimal funds. This information is incorrect and cannot be trusted. As with anything that is done quickly and for little, so will be the outcome.

In this chapter, you will learn important information before buying a flip house. This list that I have put together for you should be used a reference when actively getting ready to purchase the home. It will help you determine if this home is a diamond or a dud. If you can gather the information to answer these questions, then after you have the answer, you can look at the facts and knowledge about that house that have been exposed due to the research done. Never buy a flip house in a hurry. If the house goes under contract before you get a chance to look at it or if another contract is accepted, it is because you were not meant to have that specific house.

Houses have different issues, difficulty levels, and energies in and around them, and this is very important to consider before jumping into any large project. The right home will speak to you, and when it does, everything you do to that home will typically go exactly as it was supposed to go.

There have been times I have seen two or three buyers fighting desperately for one home, going back and forth, bidding higher and higher until one of them gets it. Either they will have paid too much and cannot make the profit they had originally estimated or they actually got the wrong home and the home's energy was not meant to be theirs. They will fix it differently than they previously wanted to because of the fact they had to bid higher to get it, which took away from fixing costs. Then, when they list the house, it sits longer than anticipated on the market because it was missing that special something that could've been included if not for the bidding war at the beginning.

Remember, the energy you bring into a home is the energy that will surround you and that home throughout the whole process. Therefore, in the case mentioned above, the buyers' energies changed because they had to pay more for the house and then had to alter what they had planned to do, so that added confusion and anxiety upfront to their project.

This is where we must take what we learned about knowledge and wisdom in chapter 2 and apply it. When researching for a property, there are common factors to consider, and those are called buy factors and sell factors. Let's discuss buy factors. They include a variety of things we need to consider when getting ready to buy our flip house:

1. What is the asking price?
2. How long has the house been on the market?
3. What is the potential for resale?
4. Will my investment be safe?
5. Will I have sufficient amount of funds to cover the remodel?
6. What is the school district?
7. What are the comparables in the area?
8. What is the inventory for sale like in this area?
9. Where are the nearest highways located?
10. Where are the local police departments, fire departments, and post offices located

in relation to this potential property?

1. What are the property taxes?
2. Are there any back taxes or liens on the property?
3. Who were the previous owners and what happened to make them sell?
4. Is this a foreclosure?
5. Will this house need extensive work or, as they call it in the real estate industry, just Cosmetic repairs?
6. If the house needs extensive repairs, what will this mean to you?

Now let's look at some sell factors:

1. Can I sell this house and make a reasonable profit?
2. Will this home sell quickly due to the area?
3. Will this home be able to accommodate enough people or a family?

4. Is there more than one bath in the home?
5. Will the buyers be happy enough with the house to be able to take on the mortgage payment, especially if it is on the higher side?
6. Will the buyers be happy with the improvements made to the home?

Huge tip: Do not go in search of a property looking for the lower price. Lower-priced properties are not always your best option.

Many circumstances depend on the property. A key factor in where the property is situated in the neighborhood is the school district. Many relocating families are trying to get into a specific school district for one reason or another, so buying closer or within walking distance will always help in the long-term portion when you list the home. This is a huge factor.

Consider the type of work you're going to have to put into it, as well as the environment around it. Many times the lower-priced properties have a great extent of work that needs to be done to get them back in shape, and then if you want to take it above and beyond that, it will up the investment you are putting into it. Older homes require a lot of time and money to be invested and usually will reveal some hidden surprises when it comes to out-of-pocket expenses.

When looking for a property, you might be thinking, *Hmm, I want to make this a quick flip*. And from the outside, it might look like it at first. To make this a quick flip, you need to look at all the aspects of the property's job before you can say this is going to be a quick one. This goes back to the second chapter, about gathering knowledge. We definitely need to do this when we have located a property that might suit our interest and accommodate our price range. Do your research here; find out all the background on the property: flood zones, basement repairs, sewer lines, and so forth. These houses are sometimes the ones that end up surprising us with that hidden broken septic system or a huge underground pool that was filled in and never maintained.

Some people go out and buy properties thinking, *I'm going to buy this house and put roughly twenty thousand dollars into it*. Quick flippers don't realize that you must look at the aspects underneath. You have to take the veil off and look behind the walls. You don't want to fall into that problem at the very end of your project when the inspector comes in. This is a worst-case scenario for everybody.

Many opportunities are available in flipping houses, but sometimes the best opportunity is not getting the cheaper priced house—trying to put roughly ten thousand to twenty thousand into it and saying it's done and listing it. Where did the passion go when this happens? Where did that initial energy go if someone sells like this and only makes about five- to ten-thousand-dollars' profit for three months of work? Is it worth it? Those kinds of houses are part-time houses. If you're looking to spend only about one to two months on it and you made yourself probably anywhere from an extra twenty-five hundred to five thousand in that time, fine. But if you end of spending more time fixing it than three months, then your profit starts to decrease—and what about the time it sits on the market ? All these things need to be considered, as they are all circumstances that happen.

4

Contractors and Estimates

Let's review a couple things we have gone over. It typically takes a good time, thirty days roughly, to find the property and do the necessary inspections. Having the inspections done cheaply on this part of the project will never benefit you. There are so many important things to be inspected in a property. Here is list of some of the biggest expenses that usually come up when flipping a property

1. The roof—This is defiantly one of the biggest and most common repairs you will have. Words of advice and wisdom: get yourself a great roofer who will be reliable, one who can say, "I don't subcontract my jobs." Getting a roofing company that does not subcontract their jobs to other crews will save you thousands of dollars on a roof. In addition, usually you can save even more if the owner is the salesman. These two things have saved me anywhere from three thousand dollars on a smaller roof job to eight thousand for a larger roof job. It makes a huge difference.

2. The foundation—Big problems can happen here. Always have a professional inspect the foundation for any cracks, shifting, bowing, caving, or sinking. As we all know, the foundation of every house is the beginning, and that whole house sits silently on that foundation, so any problems there will be urgent to address. Foundation repairs are not cheap; the minimum I have ever spent on a foundation repair was two thousand dollars, and that was just for some cracks. The foundation of everything is so important, the beginning of success. Let's pay extra attention to it, then.

3. The electrical—This is by far in the list of top expenses. For sure, this one is always my pet peeve. See, these electrical companies vary so much in their pricing that it's almost hard to trust which one is being honest. The pricing is so ridiculously up and down that it is almost unbelievable. Therefore, as mentioned concerning roofing, you need to get yourself a wonderful electrician who is trustworthy, licensed, and insured. This is one of those two peas in a pod type of relationship. I always double-check on my reliable contractors, and they know that and try to stay fair and honest. I was once given three completely different electrical bids on the same job, performing the same work with the same exact materials. It was

outrageous. I had collected the first bid for $11,750, the second for $9,500, and the final for $6,300. I went with the latter. It was from a more popular electric company too. Imagine my relief that I got to do all kinds of little extras because of that savings.

Huge tip: Always gather more than one estimate in the first portion of your house flipping. Until you know the pricing yourself, you never know who could be trying to pocket a couple of extra bucks.

4. The plumbing—This is another huge repair that you always need to take into consideration. Older houses usually require new plumbing pipes put in, and a lot of the time, a whole house of new plumbing is mandatory when you get an inspector. Typically, newer houses will need at least basic plumbing updates such as a new water heater, new fixtures, new garbage disposal, updated dishwasher pipes, and so forth. If you are doing new plumbing throughout the entire home, you can add some cool updates to the plumbing, such as a tank-less water heater, which might catch a buyer's eye. Then there is the eternal debate on piping. The new way to go is called PEX, but I like to stick with good old copper piping, and for just a little bit more, you can get a certified plumber to install that for you. Because it's usually easy to get accurate bids on plumbing, get more than one bid. This will not vary much from plumber to plumber.

    The things to look out for with your plumbing or plumbing inspections that can bring in extra costs quickly would be a septic system or well. Septic systems in older homes are usually not functioning properly because of the older materials used when first installed, or because of lack of regular maintenance, or because of excessive use. Depending on the area, different types of septic systems can be installed. In addition, there is always the option of connecting to public water supplies where perhaps there weren't any before. If you have the option of connecting to public water and sewer services, it is a great idea to take this option and not think twice about it. I have seen septic repair get extremely costly, and depending on the system or if it needs full replacement, it can run as high as twenty thousand dollars.

5. The Water Well -This is a neat type of repair and usually one of those out of the blue finds. There are options concerning this. If you have the option to keep it and just hire a well contractor to replace piping and get it working, great. If the entire well system needs to be replaced, it can get costly, so once again, if public water is available, hook up. Any well that is not in use needs to be properly capped off with cement and sealed properly. All the codes on sealing a well properly in your area should be checked with your local building code and enforcement office. At times, wells can be hazardous, so always pay attention and act on the side of caution when you have discovered one. Some wells may also be considered historic and listed in a historic register for wells. So definitely dot all your i's and cross all your t's on this one. Having other contractors on speed dial would be valuable too.

Let's discuss various contractors for situations needing addressing. As for drywall crews, the price can vary tremendously, so if you can find referrals, that is a good route to go. If you do not have a referral, you can always try calling a local apartment complex and asking the office staff for the phone number of the company they use, as well as inquiring about their painters. This is a bit of a secret, but if you are polite about it, they will hand that info right over; maybe they will even throw in the names of their carpet flooring contractors. This cuts out the middleman and gets straight to the source of the pricing. These contractors usually charge rock-bottom pricing to the apartments because of the flow of quantity they give them. Just make sure to mention who referred them and they won't try to overcharge since they have to stay comparable with the other pricing they are giving out.

Regarding foundation repair specialists, find good ones nearby who can come out quickly and do minimal repairs. Let's not try to open any foundation worms if we don't half to. Just always make sure you have the experts in on this one so they can provide you with warranties. Make sure your foundation/basement is always waterproofed and has no leaks. Any bowing or cracking from the bottom of the foundation wall to the top usually spells trouble, so call in the experts, get a proper evaluation, and then be sure you feel comfortable with the pricing and the task at hand before moving forward with a house needing foundation repairs.

Another important consideration is your HVAC contractor. Always make sure your heating and cooling systems are working properly and are up to date. There is nothing better for a buyer than walking into a home and scoring a brand-new heating and cooling system. The feel of clean warm air coming out of air ducts is nearly priceless, as are new vent covers, new thermostats, shiny new metal ductwork, and, the best part, a new furnace and AC unit. The comfort the buyer will have knowing that when it's super hot or super cold outside and not having to worry is important. All large items such as roofing, windows, siding, HVAC, electrical, and appliances come with warranties. These warranties will provide buyer reassurance every time.

Several more experts to always have picked out and ready include asphalt contractors, landscaping sod companies, structural engineers, architects, fireplace companies, a builder just in case your project takes a huge turn, and a tree company for trees that will need to be cut down or branches that need to be trimmed. Make friends with these contractors because they will help your circle grow and provide you with the confidence and support you will need.

Make or Break Your Dreams

One of my experiences in an older home I had purchased is unforgettable. I had just swooped up this beauty built in the early 1920 in a historic part of town. The pricing was incredible. It had been listed for fifty thousand dollars and was located right next door to a railroad. I remember the first time I saw it. Looking up at the home as I slowly pulled in, the feeling was strong and sudden, and I was almost in awe and then sadness. How weird to feel sadness and feelings for a home that I just saw. What was even weirder was that I had driven by that street and that home about a thousand times and never even seen it before, yet now I was having these feelings. I felt sadness when I looked at it because it was beautiful but so untaken care of; it was sparkling but dull; it was falling apart like an old swing set. I couldn't believe all the overgrown bushes, the falling branches, the trash everywhere. I couldn't believe that in the middle of this town, nobody saw this happening slowly … Well, my disbelief turned into love.

This home would have a second chance, I thought. I would bring it hope, and I would bring these old bones back to life. This was a situation I maybe should have thought about a little longer but didn't. I stepped out of the car, grabbing my cell phone and my notebook and pencil. I speed-dialed my agent and walked and talked about a mile a minute. By the time I had walked to the back of the property, she was on her way.

As we walked the entire property inside and out, I wrote my long, long list, one of the longest I had ever written when walking a property. This would be my most expensive flip yet. The whole house was completely gutted down to the enormous red oak lumber studs Yet there in the middle of all the mess was the original steps leading to the upstairs,the old fireplace and the tough original framing (all from the 1920s . I could see all the oak beams, each one probably sixteen feet long and weighing so heavily. There was not even one creak or crack; every single piece of exposed wood was sturdy and just sat in its perfect place. The listing said it was a possible teardown. Were they kidding? This house was sturdier then any house within five miles of it. Without even a single piece of carpet or heat in it, this house had such warmth.

In one far right corner of the living room sat an enormous old fireplace. I just imagined the memories that must have taken place around a crackling warm fire. On the other side, a gorgeous set of Victorian-like steps led up to a second story that was just one large open space. I immediately pictured a window seat and two bedrooms that would fit perfectly. The first floor was just one large open floorplan; it needed lots and lots of TLC. What appeared to be an old dining room led out to a tiny decrepit 1920s kitchen. The pink sink looked more like a vintage artifact than anything that would be used to wash in. I don't think I had ever seen a pink kitchen sink before. I saved that piece for sure.

What I wasn't looking forward to was the basement. I had caught a glimpse of it from upstairs because one of the back rooms on the first floor didn't even have flooring. However, I knew in my mind that the basement was always one of those deal breakers, and I didn't want it to be. In this house, I was hoping that the basement was in one piece, that the walls were standing straight, that it was not made of old concrete blocks pieced together. I was hoping for a miracle.

I moved slowly down each step as if in a slow-motion movie clip. As I came to the final steps, they took a turn and only had a piece of plywood to walk across. I saw it—the huge cold space I had been waiting to see. It was cold but not wet. It was crisp and not humid. It was old smelling but not stinky. The walls were poured concrete, thick and sturdy, just like the upstairs. They were tough and strong, with old metal posts anchoring the house up. There were all kinds of writings on the walls in spray paint, words of love and caring, hearts with initials around them. I had gotten that miracle I was hoping for. A secret wine cellar toward the right side of the basement appeared to have been used as an old coal room back in the early 1900s.

Nothing other than the walls and flooring and structural beams were salvageable in the basement, but I didn't care—my hope was fresh and renewed. Now it was time to make sure this home was mine and I could move forward with the million plans that were running through my mind. Now was the time to make my move, but how were all these extensive repairs going to fit my budget? I would have to offer much less than the asking price. Would I still be able to get it? There were many what-ifs the next day. I took my chance and did it. I offered thirty thousand for the property, twenty thousand less than they were asking. I had to; I had to fit it in my budget. I wanted the house so much that I could see all the repairs being made. I was visualizing every single room being fixed and made new again. I had the colors picked out and the landscaping pictured. Everything was done already in my mind before we even got a response back.

The next morning, my agent called with the news that they had accepted the offer. There was a twenty-eight-thousand-dollar lien on the property, and the offer would be enough for everyone to finally walk away and be happy. Yes, this couldn't have been better. Now if only the rest of the project would turn out like this, it would be smooth sailing.

Well, the rest of the project was not smooth sailing, as the case in flipping houses seldom is. There were so many bumps and pauses during the process. There were times I would walk into the house and cry and wonder if I should have it knocked it down. There were surprises every day. There was a large old buried propane tank that needed to be removed, which exposed a whole bunch of broken water pipes. The entire water piping from the house to the main street had to be replaced, four hundred feet to be exact. An old water cistern used in the day to supply water to the house needed to be removed. A buried in-ground pool that was used as an old bathhouse had to be dug up.

Day after day, month after month, we worked and pulled help from this way and that way. The city got involved; the water district got involved. It was one of my utmost difficult yet rewarding flips ever. This home had become my time, my work, my sweat, my sleep, my stress, my thoughts, my emotions. This home had gotten my love, my energy, my ideas, my happiness, and my continuous caring and attention. It was like a little puppy that needs constant attention the first couple of nights after you bring it home. That was what this home became. I called it my diamond house.

See, this diamond house got a complete shine to it. It had its brilliance arise back to life, whereas others were thinking of tearing it down to build something that would shake every time the train went by. I was thinking about its memories and history. I was thinking about who would live there and who would enjoy it as much as it had been before it was let go, before it had ended up in the wrong hands.

Let's Flip This Diamond Conclusion

When picking a property, there are so many different important things we need to consider before making that giant step and purchasing it. Always purchase with good intentions from the beginning. Always bring happiness and positive energy with you to the property. Yes, there will be times when you feel like crying or just giving up, but that's just part of the process of growing as a flipper, as an investor. Every additional house that you gain in this experience is every step closer that you achieve your goals and dreams. Each house will come with its own set of problems that you will learn from and correct. Never take a shortcut when flipping a home; the short way is not always the best and might end up costing you more in the end. No matter what anybody tells you, you're always going to have something to do with outside contractors, whether electrical, plumbing, HVAC, or asphalt or concrete.

You first have to have steady income coming in when you're flipping or, if you're deciding to quit your full-time job, have some cash saved on the side for expenses and living. During the process, you will not have money coming in from the properties, but it will be going out extremely fast. Remember to gather your lists and expenses ahead of time but know that they will never be accurate. In house flipping, there is no room for accuracy, for you do not how much you are investing in each property. It is easy to start spending money on a whole even though you have a budget,you will practically always go over your budget so budget above your budget .Don't let anybody tell you that flipping a house is easy. It's not easy. You're going to have to go through and over hills and bumps while maintaining your courage. It may be because you're deciding to do something out of your bubble or deciding to go above what you normally do as an overachiever.

Remember that you are not only flipping a house but that you are flipping a home that somebody will live in and make memories, raise a family, and grow old in. Our rewards are definitely based on how much we contribute to any project in life. You have been given a talent and a passion not just for yourself but also for the benefit of others and society. As flippers/investors, we provide work to others, we provide homes for others, and we provide stability and help to the neighborhoods. We have a job to do, and it is not just for ourselves but also for this planet.

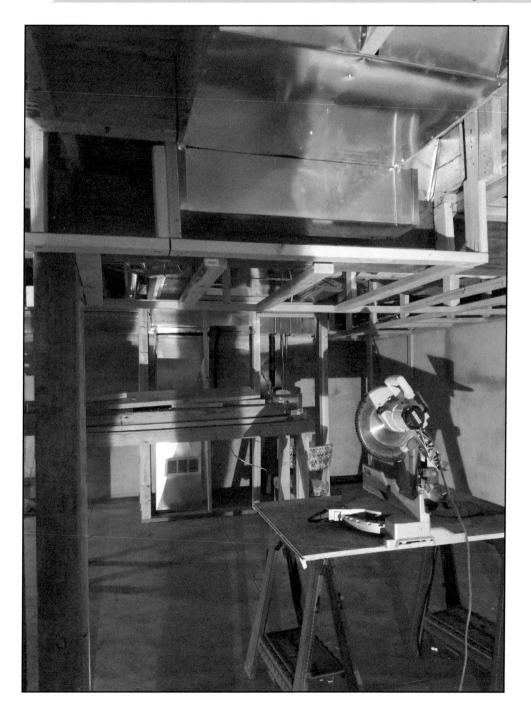

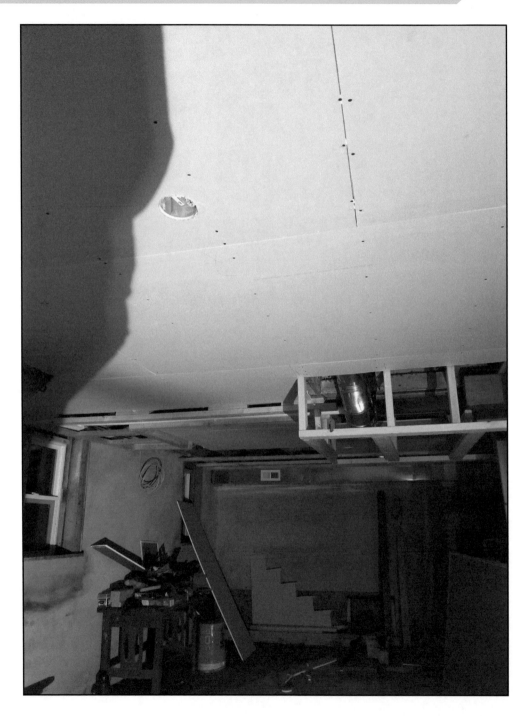

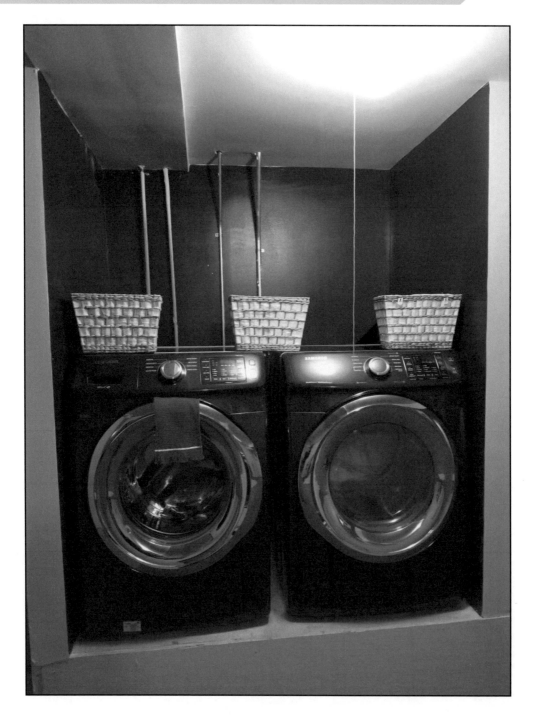

Printed in the United States
By Bookmasters